The **Richard Lewis**
Collection

25 **worship** songs

Kevin Mayhew

We hope you enjoy the music in this book.
Further copies of this and our many other books are
available from your local music shop or Christian bookshop.

In case of difficulty, please contact the publisher direct by writing to:

The Sales Department
KEVIN MAYHEW LTD
Buxhall
Stowmarket
Suffolk IP14 3BW

Phone 01449 737978
Fax 01449 737834
E-mail info@kevinmayhewltd.com

Please ask for our complete catalogue of outstanding Church Music.

First published in Great Britain in 1999 by Kevin Mayhew Ltd.

© Copyright 1999 Kevin Mayhew Ltd.

ISBN 1 84003 369 X
ISMN M 57004 554 9
Catalogue No: 1450143

0 1 2 3 4 5 6 7 8 9

Cover design by Jonathan Stroulger

Music Editor and Setter: Donald Thomson
Proof-reader: Rachel Judd

Printed and bound in Great Britain

Important Copyright Information

The Publishers wish to express their gratitude to the copyright owners who have granted permission to include their copyright material in this book. Full details are clearly indicated on the respective pages.

The **words** of the songs in this publication are covered by a **Church Copyright Licence** which allows local church reproduction on overhead projector acetates, in service bulletins, songsheets, audio/visual recording and other formats.

The **music** in this book is covered by the newly introduced 'add-on' **Music Reproduction Licence** issued by CCL (Europe) Ltd and you may photocopy the music and words of the songs in this book provided:

You hold a current Music Reproduction Licence from CCL (Europe) Ltd.

The copyright owner of the hymn or song you intend to photocopy is included in the Authorised Catalogue List which comes with your Music Reproduction Licence.

Full details of both the Church Copyright Licence and the additional Music Reproduction Licence are available from:

Christian Copyright Licensing (Europe) Ltd, PO Box 1339, Eastbourne, East Sussex, BN21 4YF. Tel: 01323 417711, fax: 01323 417722, e-mail: info@ccli.com, web: www.ccli.com.

Please note, all texts and music in this book are protected by copyright and if you do <u>not</u> possess a licence from CCL (Europe) Ltd, they may <u>not</u> be reproduced in any way for sale or private use without the consent of the copyright owner.

Every effort has been made to trace the owners of copyright material, and we hope that no copyright has been infringed. Pardon is sought and apology made if the contrary be the case, and a correction will be made in any reprint of this book.

About the Composer

Known for his work as Music Director of Kensington Temple (one of Europe's largest churches), Richard Lewis is a prolific song writer and has travelled widely giving seminars and leading worship both in the UK and overseas. While at Kensington Temple, Richard featured as worship leader on two 'live' albums, *The latter rain* and *Send revival,* both on the Kingsway Music Label. More recently Richard has released a studio album called *When I pray.* His heart is for the presence of God and to worship him through the full spectrum of biblical praise and worship.

Richard studied music at Cambridge University and Trinity College of Music, London. He is currently Worship Director of Abundant Life Family Church, Flackwell Heath, Buckinghamshire. He is married to Joy and they have two sons, Matthew and Benjamin.

Richard Lewis is available for concerts, seminars and ministry. For further information please contact:

Sploshsongs
PO Box 606
Maidenhead
Berkshire
SL6 1WS

E-mail: taketheplunge@sploshsongs.freeserve.co.uk
Website: www.sploshsongs.freeserve.co.uk

Foreword

At 6 am one September morning in 1994 I was awakened by a song! I had to get up and write it down. As I tried to go back to sleep again, another song started to come which I also wrote down. This one was called *The latter rain* – we sang it that evening at the Kensington Temple Holy Spirit meeting. It became for us a theme-song of the great move of the Holy Spirit that was sweeping across Europe at that time. Since then song writing has been a useful tool in leading people into the presence of God through Praise and Worship. Some songs have come in an instant; others have taken years to write. This collection represents some of the songs written during my time as Music Director of Kensington Temple, Notting Hill Gate (1994-1998). The songs range from thanksgiving (*We're so thankful* – co-written with Chris Cartwright), through praise (*High praises*) to intimate worship (*Lord, we long to see your glory*).

I would like to dedicate this book to my wife who has so faithfully applied the 'wife-test' to so many of my musical musings and saved God's people from much suffering. The Lord's joy has been my strength!

RICHARD LEWIS
MAIDENHEAD, MARCH 1999

O God, my heart is steadfast:
I will sing and give praise, even with my glory.
Awake, lute and harp!
I will awaken the dawn.

Ps. 108:1-2

1 As the deer pants

Your waves of love

Words and Music: Richard Lewis

Rhythmically

As the deer pants for the wa - ter, so my

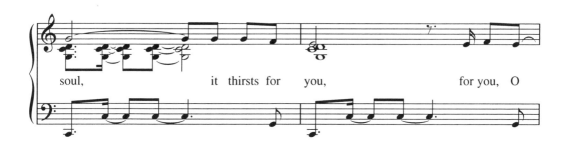

soul, it thirsts for you, for you, O

God, for you, O God.

As the When can I come be-fore

2 Come to the power

A mighty fortress

Words and Music: Richard Lewis

3 Father, we adore you

We worship you

Words and Music: Richard Lewis

4 Give us passion for the Lamb of God

Passion for Jesus

Words and Music: Richard Lewis

5 He rides on the wings of the wind

Consuming fire

Words and Music: Richard Lewis

2. His hair is as white as the snow, his eyes are a flame of fire;
   holy is he, holy is he.
   his feet are like glowing bronze, his voice like the many waters;
   holy is he, holy is he.

6 He's the image of the invisible God

Supernatural God

Words and Music: Richard Lewis

1. He's the im - age of the in - vi - si - ble God. He is the first - born o - ver all cre - a - tion, for by him were all things cre - a - ted in earth and

2. Ever living, he's the first and the last.
   Alpha and Omega shed his blood on a cross.
   He's the Amen, witness faithful and true,
   the word of God's power – he died for you.
   Whether thrones or dominions, prinicipalities or powers,
   all things were created by him.
   Whether thrones or dominions, principalities or powers,
   all things were created by him and for him.

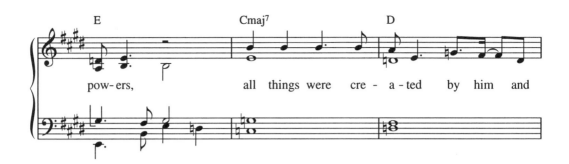

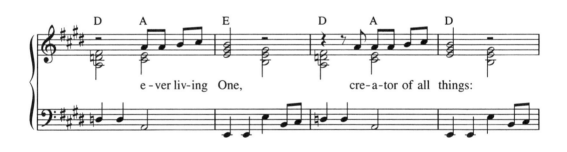

7 High praises

Words and Music: Richard Lewis

8 Holy, holy, Lord God Almighty

Words and Music: Richard Lewis

9 I will awaken the dawn

Words and Music: Richard Lewis

10 I will testify

Words and Music: Richard Lewis

he has paid the price with his ne - ver end - ing love.

Deep as the o -cean, high as the

high - est heav'n a -bove, wide as the east is from the west

is your great love. is your great love.

11 Lift up your heads, O ye gates

Words and Music: Richard Lewis

12 Lord, we long to see your glory

Words and Music: Richard Lewis

13 More, Lord

Words and Music: Richard Lewis

More, Lord, give us more of your Spi-rit, give us more; we o-pen our

hearts. More, Lord, give us more of your Spi-rit in our

lives; we yield them to you. Give us more of your Spi - rit, give us

more of the Son, give us more of the Fa - ther, come and

fill ev - 'ry one. I re - ceive your Spi - rit, I re - ceive your love, I re -

ceive the pow - er of the Lord God a - bove. Glo - ri -

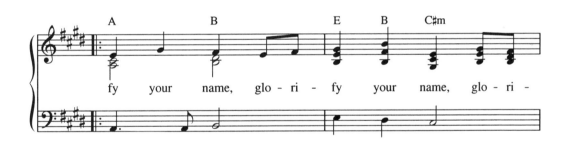

fy your name, glo - ri - fy your name, glo - ri -

fy your name in all the earth. Glo - ri -

14 Not unto us, O Lord

Words and Music: Richard Lewis

Brightly

Not un - to us, not un - to us, O Lord be the

glo - ry, but to your name for the sake of your mer - cy and

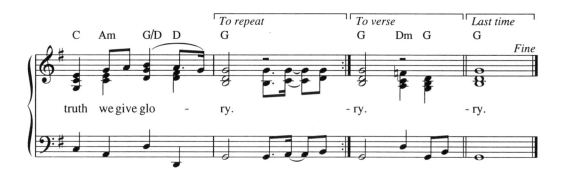

truth we give glo - ry. - ry. - ry.

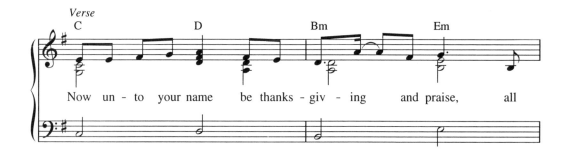

Now un - to your name be thanks - giv - ing and praise, all

hon - our and pow - er and do - min - ion. May the

in - crease of your reign be made ma - ni - fest a - mong us, the

har - vest of re - vi - val in your king - dom.

15 Set me as a seal

It burns like fire

Words and Music: Richard Lewis

Thoughtfully

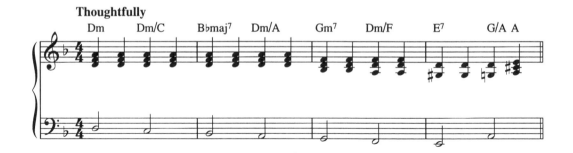

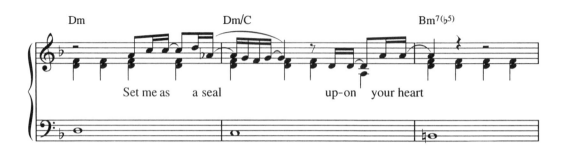

Set me as a seal up-on your heart

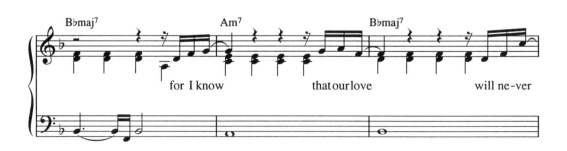

for I know that our love will ne-ver

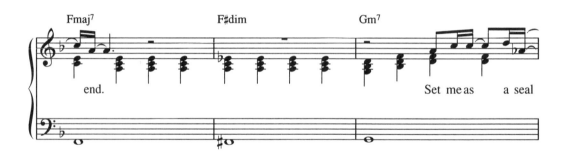

end. Set me as a seal

up-on your heart   for I know

that our love   will ne-ver end.

For love   is as   strong   as death,

its jea-lou-sy is cruel as the grave.   For love   is as

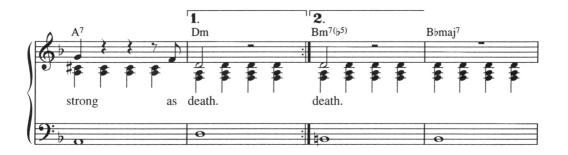

strong   as death.   death.

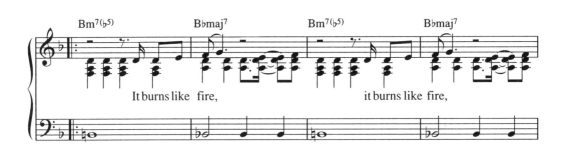

It burns like fire, it burns like fire,

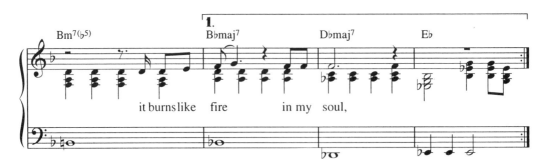

1.

it burns like fire in my soul,

2.

fire in my soul, in my

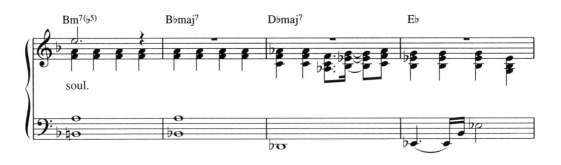

soul.

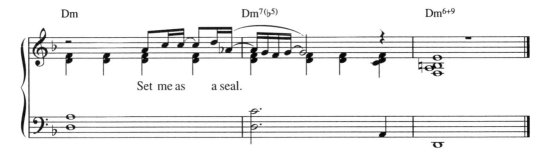

Set me as a seal.

16 The angels around your throne

Words and Music: Richard Lewis

2. The angels around your throne,
   they cry 'Worthy is the Lamb.' *etc.*

17 The Lord is marching out

Words and Music: Richard Lewis

18 There's an awesome sound

Send revival

Words and Music: Richard Lewis

2. All creation sings of the Lamb of glory
   who laid down his life for all the world.
   What amazing love, that the King of heaven
   should be crucified, stretching out his arms,
   his arms of love, his arms of love.

19 The weapons of our warfare

Words and Music: Richard Lewis

The wea-pons of our war-fare are migh-ty in God. The God to the pull-ing down, to the pull-ing down of the strong-holds of the e-ne-my.

We are wag-ing war not a-gainst flesh and

blood, but we fight the e-vil spi - rit pow'rs. The world don't un-der-

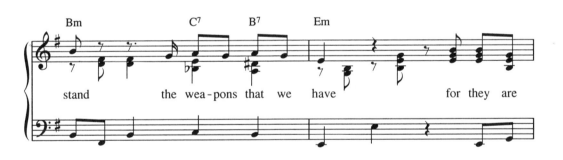

stand the wea-pons that we have for they are

pow'r-ful in Je-sus Christ our Lord. The

20 To the highest place

Words and Music: Richard Lewis

21 We ask you, O Lord

The latter rain

Words and Music: Richard Lewis

22 We're so thankful to you

Thank you, Lord

Words and Music: Chris Cartwright and Richard Lewis

1. We're so thank-ful to you, we're so grate-ful for the things you've done, that you died for us on the cross, such a pain-ful death, that you paid the price for us, you paid the price for us. And we say thank you, Lord. We say thank you,

Lord. We say thank you for what you have

done. And we say thank you, Lord. We say

thank you, Lord. We say thank you for the things you have

done. 2. It's so

2. It's so wonderful that you rose,
   victorious over death and hell.
   All authority is now yours,
   and the Comforter
   you have sent in fullness to us,
   you have come to us.

23 When I pray

Fire fall

Words and Music: Richard Lewis

2. For my praise, it burns like incense,
   and my prayers rise to your throne,
   they release fire from the altar,
   and the Devil cannot stand,
   and the Devil cannot stand,
   and the Devil cannot stand
   when I pray.

24 You are the anchor and foundation

Never let me go

Words and Music: David Grant, Carrie Grant and Richard Lewis

2. You are the King in all your glory,
   you are the Lamb of victory,
   you are the mercy-giver
   and you deliver
   all the grace I'll ever need.

25 You are the Lord of heaven

Words and Music: Richard Lewis

With mystery

You are the Lord of hea - ven, you are the King of ho - ly Zi - on

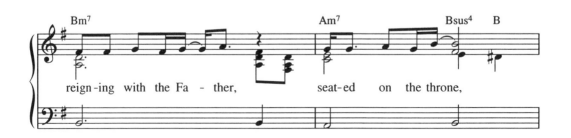

reign-ing with the Fa - ther, seat-ed on the throne,

you are a priest for e - ver, you are my great in-ter-ces - sor;

an-gels bow be-fore you, wor-ship you a-lone.

Je - sus, how love - ly you are:

King of peace and right - eous-ness, we wor - ship you.

we wor - ship you.

The **Richard Lewis** Collection

Acetate masters

As the deer pants for the water,
so my soul, it thirsts for you,
for you, O God, for you, O God.
(Repeat)

When can I come before you
and see your face?
My heart and my flesh cry out
for the living God, for the living God.
Deep calls to deep
at the thunder of your waterfalls.
Your heart of love
is calling out to me.
By this I know that I am yours
and you are mine.
Your waves of love are breaking over me.
Your waves of love are breaking over me.
Your waves of love are breaking over me.

Richard Lewis

© Copyright 1997 Kingsway's Thankyou Music, PO Box 75, Eastbourne,
East Sussex, BN23 6NW, UK. Used by permission.

CCL Licence No. _____

Come to the power, the power of the
living God,
his name is higher, higher than any
other name.
Mighty Jehovah, awesome deliverer,
his power is greater, greater than any
principality.
A mighty fortress is our God,
he sits enthroned in the heavens,
the Lord of hosts is he.
A mighty fortress is our God,
he sits enthroned in the heavens,
he reigns in majesty.
A mighty fortress is our God,
he sits enthroned in the heavens,
the Lord of hosts is he.
A mighty fortress is our God,
he sits enthroned in the heavens,
he reigns in majesty, in majesty.

Richard Lewis

Father, we adore you,
reigning in eternity.
Father, we adore you,
awesome in your majesty,
awesome in your majesty.
We worship you, with all our hearts,
we worship you, God most high,
we worship you, and we lay our lives
    before you
as a living sacrifice.
Lead us to the secret place of thunder,
lead us to the secret place of praise.
Lead us to the secret place of thunder,
lead us to the secret place of praise.

Give us passion, for the Lamb of God,
who takes away the sins of the world.
Lord, give us passion.
Greater love has no man than to lay
    down his life for his friends.
Lord, give us passion for Jesus,
passion for his love that's strong as
    death.
Passion that burns with your holy fire,
    passion for you.
Let the church rise up with new
    determination,
that the world might know the power of
    the cross,
and your gospel be preached in every
    nation,
salvation to the lost.
Passion for Jesus, passion for Jesus,
passion for Jesus, passion for you.

Richard Lewis

© Copyright 1996 Kingsway's Thankyou Music, PO Box 75, Eastbourne,
East Sussex, BN23 6NW, UK. Used by permission.
CCL Licence No. _____

He rides on the wings of the wind,
his chariot the clouds of heaven.
Holy is he, holy is he.
He's clothed in a garment of light,
his messengers are flames of fire.
Holy is he, holy is he.

It's an awesome thing, to be in his
   presence,
oh how I need his Spirit's work in me.
Consuming fire, my heart's desire,
come Spirit fire, burn a fresh in me.
Consuming fire, my heart's desire,
come Spirit fire, burn a fresh in me.

His hair is as white as the snow,
his eyes are a flame of fire.
Holy is he, holy is he.
His feet are like glowing bronze,
his voice like the many waters.
Holy is he, holy is he.

Richard Lewis

He's the image of the invisible God,
he's the first born over all creation,
for by him were all things created
in earth and heaven, seen and unseen.
Whether thrones or dominions,
   principalities or powers,
all things were created by him.
Whether thrones or dominions,
   principalities or powers,
all things were created by him and for
   him.

Supernatural God, ever living One,
creator of all things we worship you.
Supernatural God, ever living One,
creator of all things we worship you.

Ever living, he's the first and the last,
Alpha and Omega, shed his blood on a
cross.
He's the Amen, witness faithful and true,
the Word of God's power, he died for
you.
Whether thrones or dominions,
principalities or powers,
all things were created by him.
Whether thrones or dominions,
principalities or powers,
all things were created by him and for
him.

Supernatural God, ever living One,
creator of all things we worship you.
Supernatural God, ever living One,
creator of all things we worship you.

Richard Lewis

High praises, high praises,
high praises, high praises,
high praises, high praises,
these are the praises of heaven.
(Repeat)

Legions of angels in bright array,
worship the great 'I AM'.
Singing with joy of that glorious day,
when he will come to reign.
Singing . . .

Glory and honour and pow'r to him
who's seated upon the throne.
This is the everlasting song
that they sing to him alone.
Singing . . .

Richard Lewis

Holy, holy, Lord God Almighty,
who was, and who is, and is to come.
Holy, holy, Lord God Almighty,
who was, and who is, and is to come.
All the angels cry, 'Holy',
all the angels cry, 'Holy',
all the angels cry, 'Holy is your name.'
Holy is your name. Holy is your name.
Holy is your name. Holy is your name.

Richard Lewis
© Copyright 1997 Kingsway's Thankyou Music, PO Box 75, Eastbourne,
East Sussex, BN23 6NW, UK. Used by permission.
CCL Licence No. _____

I will awaken the dawn,
I will sing praises till the heavens come
   down.
I won't give up till you come,
I won't give up until the fire is falling.
(Repeat)

You are the Lily of the Valley,
you are the hope when hope has gone.
You are the light that shines for ever.
Jehovah is your name
and I've never been the same,
since I put my trust in you.

Jehovah your love will never end.
Jehovah your love will never end.
(Repeat)

Richard Lewis

© Copyright 1998 Sploshsongs. Administered by CopyCare, PO Box 77,
Hailsham, East Sussex, BN27 3EF, UK. Used by permission.

CCL Licence No. _____

I will testify, to the Saviour whom I love,
who laid down his life, for all my guilt
and shame.
He was crucified, to take away my sin,
he has paid the price, with his never
ending love.
Deep as the ocean, high as the highest
heaven above,
wide as the east is from the west, is your
great love.
Deep as the ocean, high as the highest
heaven above,
wide as the east is from the west, is your
great love.

Richard Lewis

© Copyright 1998 Sploshsongs. Administered by CopyCare, PO Box 77,
Hailsham, East Sussex, BN27 3EF, UK. Used by permission.

CCL Licence No. _____

Lift up your heads, O you gates,
be lifted up, O ancient doors,
that the King of glory may come in,
that the King of glory may come in.
(Repeat)

Who is this King of glory?
The Lord strong and mighty.
Who is this King of glory?
The Lord strong and mighty in battle.
Worthy is he to receive all honour,
worthy is he to receive all praise,
worthy is he to receive the glory.
Glory to God, glory to God, glory to
    God.
(Repeat)

Lord, we long to see your glory,
gaze upon your lovely face.
Holy Spirit, come among us,
lead us to that secret place.
Holy God, we long to see your glory,
to touch your holy majesty, O Lord.
Holy God, let us stay in your presence,
and worship at your feet for evermore.
Holy God. Holy God.

Richard Lewis

More, Lord, give us more of your Spirit,
give us more, we open our hearts.
More, Lord, give us more of your Spirit
   in our lives,
we yield them to you, give us more of
   your Spirit,
give us more of the Son, give us more of
   the Father,
come and fill ev'ry one.
I receive your Spirit, I receive your love,
I receive the power of the Lord God
   above.

Glorify your name, glorify your name,
glorify your name in all the earth.
(Repeat)

Richard Lewis

Not unto us, not unto us,
O Lord, be the glory,
but to your name, for the sake of your
     mercy and truth,
we give glory.
(Repeat)

Now unto your name be thanksgiving
   and praise,
all honour and power and dominion.
May the increase of your reign
be made manifest among us,
the harvest of revival in your kingdom.

Richard Lewis

Set me as a seal upon your heart,
for I know that our love will never end.
Set me as a seal upon your heart,
for I know that our love will never end.

For love is as strong as death,
it's jealousy is cruel as the grave,
for love is as strong as death.
(Repeat)

It burns like fire, it burns like fire,
it burns like fire, in my soul.
It burns like fire, it burns like fire,
it burns like fire, in my soul, in my soul.
Set me as a seal.

Richard Lewis

© Copyright 1998 Sploshsongs. Administered by CopyCare, PO Box 77,
Hailsham, East Sussex, BN27 3EF, UK. Used by permission.

CCL Licence No. _____

The angels around your throne they cry,
'Holy is the Lamb'.
The angels around your throne they cry,
'Holy is the Lamb',
so we sing holy, holy, holy, holy is the
Lamb,
so we sing holy, holy, holy, holy is the
Lamb.

The angels around your throne they cry,
'Worthy is the Lamb'.
The angels around your throne they cry,
'Worthy is the Lamb',
so we sing worthy, worthy, worthy,
worthy is the Lamb,
so we sing worthy, worthy, worthy,
worthy is the Lamb.

The Lord is marching out, like a mighty
    man of war,
stirring up his zeal, with a shout and a
    roar.
The Lord is marching out, like a mighty
    man of war,
stirring up his zeal, with a shout and a
    roar.
And he'll triumph . . . . triumph,
triumph over his foes.

Jesus (Jesus).
Jesus (Jesus).

Richard Lewis

There's an awesome sound on the winds
   of heaven,
mighty thunder-clouds in the skies
   above.
The immortal King who will reign for
   ever
is reaching out with his arms of love,
his arms of love, his arms of love.

All creation sings of the Lamb of glory
who laid down his life for all the world.
What amazing love, that the King of
   heaven
should be crucified, stretching out his
   arms,
his arms of love, his arms of love.

Send revival to this land,
fill this nation with your love.
Send revival to this land,
fill this nation with your love.

Richard Lewis

The weapons of our warfare are mighty
in God.
The weapons of our warfare are mighty
in God.
To the pulling down, to the pulling
down,
of the strongholds of the enemy.
We are waging war not against flesh and
blood,
but we fight evil spirit powers.
The world don't understand the weapons
that we have
for they are powerful in Jesus Christ our
Lord.

Richard Lewis

To the highest place, to the majestic
   glory,
he is lifted up, by the God of love.
King of heaven is he, and a high priest
   for ever,
interceding for us, at the throne of God.
His name is Jesus, Emmanuel, God is
   with us,
Jesus, wonderful Counsellor.

O how we love him,
O how we love him,
O how we love him,
great intercessor.
(Repeat)

Our advocate in heaven, high priest for
   ever.
in the order of Melchizedek.

Richard Lewis

We ask you, O Lord, for the rain of your
    Spirit,
we ask you, O Lord, for the rain of your
    Spirit,
for now is the time, for now is the time,
of the latter rain, of the latter rain.
(Repeat)

Send your rain, cleanse us by your word,
let us be your pure and radiant bride.
Make us strong, prepare us for revival,
let us see the nations turn their hearts,
let us see the nations turn their hearts,
let us see the nations turn their hearts
    to you.

Send your rain, mercy from heaven,
send your rain, the grace of your Son.
Send your rain, word of your power,
send your rain, come fill everyone.
(Repeat)

We're so thankful to you,
we're so grateful, for the things you've
  done,
that you died for us on the cross,
such a painful death,
that you paid the price for us,
you paid the price for us.

And we say thank you, Lord.
We say thank you, Lord.
We say thank you, for what you have
  done.
And we say thank you, Lord.
We say thank you, Lord.
We say thank you, for the things you
  have done.

It's so wonderful that you rose,
victorious over death and hell,
all authority is now yours.
And the comforter,
you have sent in fullness to us,
you have come to us.

Chris Cartwright & Richard Lewis

© Copyright 1994 Kingsway's Thankyou Music, PO Box 75, Eastbourne,
East Sussex, BN23 6NW, UK. Used by permission.

CCL Licence No. _____

When I pray, the Devil trembles,
when I sing, the strongholds fall,
for I know my God is for me,
and the Devil cannot stand,
and the Devil cannot stand,
and the Devil cannot stand,
when I pray.

Fire fall! Fire fall!
And release the kingdom of the living
    God.
(Repeat)

For my praise, it burns like incense,
and my prayers, rise to your throne,
they release fire from the altar,
and the Devil cannot stand,
and the Devil cannot stand,
and the Devil cannot stand,
when I pray.

Richard Lewis

Oh, oh, oh, oh.
Oh, oh, oh, oh.

You are the anchor and foundation,
you are the rock that will not roll.
You are the one provider, the purifier
and the lover of my soul.

Jesus, Saviour, you let me know,
you made a covenant of love with me
and you'll never let me go.
Oh, never let me go, never let me go,
never let me go, never let me go,
never let me go.

You are the King in all your glory,
you are the Lamb of victory,
you are the mercy-giver and you deliver
all the grace I'll ever need.

David Grant, Carrie Grant & Richard Lewis

© Copyright 1996 / Copyright Control Kingsway's Thankyou Music, PO Box 75, Eastbourne,
East Sussex, BN23 6NW, UK. Used by permission.

CCL Licence No. _____

You are the Lord of heaven,
you are the King of holy Zion,
reigning with the Father,
seated on the throne.
You are a priest for ever,
you are my great intercessor,
angels bow before you, worship you
    alone.

Jesus, how lovely you are,
King of peace and righteousness,
we worship you.
(Repeat)

Richard Lewis

© Copyright 1998 Sploshsongs. Administered by CopyCare, PO Box 77,
Hailsham, East Sussex, BN27 3EF, UK. Used by permission.

CCL Licence No. _____

The recordings listed opposite are available from your local Christian bookshop, or direct from the following sources:

Latter Rain
Send Revival

Available from:
Kingsway Communications
P.O. Box 75
Eastbourne
East Sussex
BN23 6NW

Tel: 01323 410930
Fax: 01323 411970

When I pray

Available from:
ICC
Silverdale Road
Eastbourne
East Sussex
BN20 7AB

Tel: 01323 643341
Fax: 01323 649240
E-mail: icc@mistral.co.uk

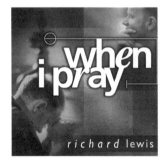

Index of First Lines, Titles and Recordings

This index gives the first line of each song. If a song is known by an alternative title, this is also given, but indented and in italics. A key to the recordings will be found at the end of this index.

	No.	Rec.
A mighty fortress	2	1
As the deer pants	1	3
Come to the power	2	1
Consuming fire	5	1
Father, we adore you	3	1
Fire fall	23	1
Give us passion for the Lamb of God	4	2
He rides on the wings of the wind	5	1
He's the image of the invisible God	6	1
High praises	7	2
Holy, holy, Lord God Almighty	8	3
It burns like fire	15	1
I will awaken the dawn	9	1
I will testify	10	1
Lift up your heads, O ye gates	11	2
Lord, we long to see your glory	12	3
More, Lord	13	1
Never let me go	24	2
Not unto us, O Lord	14	2
Passion for Jesus	4	2
Send revival	18	3
Set me as a seal	15	1
Supernatural God	6	1
Thank you, Lord	22	2
The angels around your throne	16	2
The latter rain	21	2
The Lord is marching out	17	2
There's an awesome sound	18	3
The weapons of our warfare	19	1
To the highest place	20	1
We ask you, O Lord	21	2
We're so thankful to you	22	2
We worship you	3	1
When I pray	23	1
You are the anchor and foundation	24	2
You are the Lord heaven	25	1
Your waves of love	1	3

Key to recordings:

1 *When I pray* (ICC)
2 *Latter rain* (Kingsway)
3 *Send revival* (Kingsway)

See opposite for further details.

2159m   nmo